A SPIRIT DAUGHTER WORKBOOK

WRITTEN BY
JILL WINTERSTEEN

FOR THE BLUE MOON

WEDNESDAY, AUGUST 30TH

6:36 PM PT

THE BLUE MOON

This August, we have two Full Moons. The first, occurring on August 1 in the sign of Aquarius, is known as the Sturgeon Moon. The second Full Moon of October falls in Pisces and is a Blue Moon. It's also a Super Moon. While the Moon will not actually be blue, it is a rare event to have two Full Moons in one month, bookending the energy of August. Expect this day to be filled with magic, serendipity, and revelations.

Full Moons show us what is normally hidden. In the bright light of the Moon, we can see further into ourselves and those around us. We can understand things from a different perceptive, and with this awareness, we can release them. Full Moons occur from an opposition of the Sun and the Moon as we on Earth sit in the middle of these two celestial bodies. When we look up in the night sky, we can see the full illumination of the Moon as the Sun's rays reflect her brilliance. This opposition feels intense on our energetic system, as it brings out places we need to shift to change our vibration. The Full Moon allows us to understand ourselves more deeply and see what needs attention in our frequency.

The Full Moon is flavored or themed by the zodiac constellation in which it is positioned. This energy further directs our focus and helps us understand how we may be aligned with the sign's higher or lower frequencies. Every vibration, including those from the stars, has a high or low side we can align with in our energetic body. We'll go deeper into discussing the low and high sides of Pisces later in this workbook, but for now, think of it as a spectrum of energy. On one end, we have the low side, and the other, the high side. As we work with the Full Moon, we can release and shift away from the lower frequencies of the sign involved, making it possible to embrace and align with the higher frequencies.

Each Full Moon brings us an opportunity to shift our vibration in a very specific way. The Pisces Full Moon reveals different energies within us compared to the Aries or Aquarius Full Moon. Each Full Moon brings its own set of vibrations. As we journey from one Full Moon to another, through the astrological signs, we touch on every aspect of our life and personality. We create a blueprint to shift our vibration one Full Moon at a time until we are vibrating at the highest level possible in all areas of life.

The Blue Moon brings us an extra dose of magic. While a Blue Moon isn't blue, the symbology of the color blue endures. Blue is the color of communication. It is associated with the throat chakra and signifies the expression of our most authentic truths. Blue Moons can shed light on how we communicate with ourselves and others. They ask us if we are speaking our most profound truths or suppressing our authentic voice. The rarity of the Blue Moon and its power to connect us to our voices give it a greater ability to lower the veil between the conscious and the subconscious minds. We can communicate with our unconscious thoughts, patterns, and feelings on a deeper level during a Blue Moon. It's a time to access the energies that lie dormant within us that are asking to be seen and heard.

PISCES BLUE MOON

The Pisces Full Moon is perhaps one of the more mystical Full Moons of the year. As a water sign, Pisces adds an extra element of intuition, femininity, and transcendence to this Full Moon. It brings out our creativity, our capacity to heal, and our willingness to dive deep into the unknown. Pisces represents the ocean—vast, boundless, and connected to everything. This energy is the thread that ties the Universe together. It reminds us that we are one with everything. This Full Moon is a time to relax, expand, and let go of control as we all ride the waves into a higher consciousness.

In working with the Pisces energy, we have the opportunity to go beyond the superficial nature of life and open ourselves to something much more substantial. Pisces opens the pathway to understanding life from a different vantage point. It grants us a higher awareness that soothes our everyday anxieties and teaches us that everything truly is meant to be. Pisces reminds us that there are many levels of awareness and consciousness. We are conscious of many things and are becoming more aware each day. People are waking up to realties that are not their own. We are becoming more and more conscious of how others experience the world and how that experience may differ greatly from our own. Through our technology, we are more connected than ever to other people on this planet. This connection can serve to create more awareness or it can serve to distract us.

This Pisces Full Moon is an opportunity to release the many energies that distract us or make us forget our potential. It can be easy to get lost in a sea of stimuli that demand our attention. We are aware of so many things these days, and it is easy to become hypnotized by the onslaught of visual cues we encounter. While technology has brought us information at lightning speed, it also can overwhelm our senses to the point where we become numb or caught in a trance of light and sound. While it can be good to remain current on the events of the world, this Full Moon encourages you to take your awareness to another level. It asks that you limit your distractions, especially the ones causing emotional disturbances.

PISCES BLUE MOON

It asks that you recognize what is overwhelming your senses and step back to give yourself space. Instead of feeling immersed in a sea of energy, become an observer—connected but unaffected. In this space find the higher meaning to every experience and a deeper understanding of your journey. What are you really here to experience? How can you raise your awareness while staying connected to the world?

Part of the higher awareness offered by Pisces is an understanding of the flow of your life and what it means to be in it. We are each composed of energy on a path of evolution. This energy is connected to everyone and everything in the Universe. We are the stars, the ocean, and the Moon. The individual energy that makes up our bodies, minds, and consciousness is on a mission. It wants to evolve and has chosen this manifestation for its next evolutionary journey. In order for our energy to gather what it needs to transform, we go through different experiences—both pleasant and unpleasant. Every experience is somehow connected to the evolution of our energy. This statement can be a hard pill to swallow, as it includes the myriad of experiences life offers, including death itself. Pisces, though, teaches that there is no death—only the redistribution of energy. We are human and we suffer. We have desires, we have loved ones, and we have heartache. Life can bring the most painful experiences and the most beautiful ones—and sometimes it brings both in the same package.

On this Full Moon, the Pisces energy invites you to rise above your experiences and feel into the vastness of your energy. It asks that you take a leap in consciousness and try to understand that everything you've experienced is serving your evolution in some way. It is teaching you something, and even though it may be heart wrenching, it is helping your energy evolve. It is helping you reach enlightenment, one experience at a time. Understanding this will also help you heal from the pain life hands you. Also, the more experiences you embrace as part of your evolution, the more you will receive, putting you in the flow of your life. Being in the flow means you attract what you need for your energy to evolve in this lifetime. It means you are running into the people who can guide you, finding the information you need to gain new perspectives, and attracting the frequencies that align you with your energy's journey. Being in the flow is something you can feel. Every step feels aligned and brings you something that helps you grow. It does not always mean that everything works out how you want it to, but every experience does serve your growth and evolution.

Pisces reminds you this Full Moon, and always, that when you are in the flow, you do not need to force things. You do not need to control or perfect anything. The more you let go of attachments and expectations, the more you will feel aligned with your life. You do not need to do anything to be in the flow of your life. You just need to release the barriers within you that prevent you from receiving what you need. This release is the work of this Full Moon. It starts when you raise your awareness to accept all experiences and understand the larger vision of your energy. Over this Full Moon, break free of your distractions and travel to a deeper level of understanding of the world around you. See past the superficial goings-on of the world and start to see the energy that comprises it all. See the pathways of evolution and the patterns that form. Feel your connection to the Universe and know that through this connection you are able to receive everything you need for your soul's journey. Work to let go of how you expect life to be and start accepting how it is. In this acceptance, see the beauty of your soul shining through the light of the Moon.

PISCES MOON X VIRGO SUN

Every Full Moon brings us the opportunity to work with its counterpart where the Sun is positioned. Over the Pisces Full Moon, we are also working with Virgo's energy. These energies exist on a spectrum. On one end, we have the extreme, or shadow sides, of Virgo. On the other end, we have the extreme sides of Pisces. In the middle, we have a beautiful mix of the highest sides of both energies, where we can benefit from the compilation of both vibrations. The key is to become aware of when we are aligned with the extreme, or shadow, sides of either vibration and shift them. We can then step into the higher realm of both energies and harness them to manifest our visions.

Every zodiac sign carries certain archetypal vibrations. These are energies that exist in the Universe and can become part of anyone's energetic field. We all hold the seeds for the frequencies of Pisces and Virgo. We all have these energies in our natal chart, and either the low or high side of these frequencies can become predominant at any time. If you find yourself aligning with the lower frequencies of any sign, know that this is not personal to you. It can happen to anyone, and there is nothing wrong with you. You are simply attached to a certain vibration of the Universe, and that attachment can be released on a Full Moon.

Pisces and Virgo, like all opposing signs, have some interesting similarities. They are both highly feminine signs, meaning they enhance our ability to receive energy. They both carry the vibrations of great healers. They are both highly intuitive and heighten our intuition. They are also both signs of service. Virgo serves the world with its keen insights and discernment, while Pisces serves the Universe with its ability to connect all energies throughout space and time. They are also both mutable signs, helping us transition from one frequency to another.

These signs hold some differences, though, and this is where we can also find their shadows. Pisces is boundless like the ocean. It sees no separation between us and other people. Virgo knows only separation. It seeks to constantly filter, organize, and refine energy. Where Pisces can lack boundaries, Virgo can develop too many. Pisces can also become too malleable, not taking any shape, position, or perspective. It can go with the flow a little too much and end up overly passive in the world. Virgo can become too inflexible and rigid. It can seek to overly define situations. In that definition, it loses the magic of spontaneity and serendipity. Virgo can become misaligned with the flow of the Universe by trying to control it or box it in with perfectionism.

When we align with the lower vibrations of Virgo, we construct too many walls in life. We seek to organize and control every aspect of our world. We forget to leave room for the impossible and things we can't quite imagine. We become inflexible to spontaneous changes brought on by the Universe. We also forget that we are constantly co-creating our reality with the cosmos and instead try to take charge of too many situations. We lose the ability to pause and observe the space between an event and our response. Instead, we launch straight in with our demands, need for validation, and attempts to control every outcome. We are not comfortable in the space of not knowing and, in turn, are not comfortable with ourselves. We may even become restless in our own bodies, unable to digest the energy around us.

If you find yourself aligning with the lower energies of Virgo, harness that need to control into setting up a routine of self-care. Carve out time to meditate, be one with the Universe, and connect with your energy subconsciously. Seek to create space in your life and observe your reactions with compassion. Let go of the need to create a perfect life for yourself and instead embrace the chaos that is necessary to cultivate a wonderful life. As you develop a pause before your reactions to the world, feel your intuition. Let it lead you away from logical answers and instead harness your energy to feel the path forward. Trust yourself, trust the process of your life, and know that you don't need all the answers to make decisions that move you forward. You can wander into the unknown and let the Universe surprise you with the unimaginable.

Conversely, when we align with the lower vibrations of Pisces, we become passive and lack boundaries. We merge our energy with everyone we meet and take on their pain. We become overly empathic and overly sensitive to the needs of others. We also forget to observe our reactions and instead become overwhelmed with emotions and energy. We cannot discern what is ours and what does not belong to us. We also forgot about our power to create our lives. We leave everything up to the Universe and become passive participants. We disempower ourselves to make decisions. We also forget about our responsibility to remove internal barriers. We expect that life will flow without us having to work on ourselves to heal, evolve, and be accountable for our lives.

If you find yourself aligning with the lower energies of Pisces, spend time in deep meditation. Feel your intuition, but also feel your emotions. Feel what is yours versus what you are carrying for someone else. Also, feel your power to co-create your reality. While you do want to leave space for serendipity and magic, you also want to declare your visions to the Universe. It's important to be ok with them evolving differently than you imagined, but it's also important to know what you want in the first place. As you meditate on a deeper level, you will gain the insight of higher consciousness, which teaches you to do the work needed to manifest your dreams while being detached from any outcome. You will also create more space before any response, enabling you to process what just unfolded and understand its higher meaning in the context of your evolution.

Creating more space in your conscious mind will also help you understand when boundaries are needed and how to develop them energetically and internally. Boundaries can protect your peace and help you align more with the flow of your life. When you can insulate your energy from intrusive vibrations set out to invade your space, you can then align with your intuition and higher visions to a greater degree. Boundaries are needed, especially when you feel highly sensitive or overstimulated by the world. These boundaries may look like time away from your phone, limits on how much energy you share with others, who you let in your life, and how much time you spend practicing healing or giving. They can also be practices like encasing yourself with white light when helping others process their experiences or when going out into the world. The more energetic and sensitive you become through meditation, the more boundaries you need. We do not live in a world that respects energetic sensitivity, especially if you live in a city. You need to prioritize taking care of yourself, or the world around you will overstimulate your system, causing you to feel emotional, reactive, and powerless.

As you work with the many energies, this Pisces Full Moon brings, look for the full integration of the higher energies of Pisces and Virgo. Seek to feel your intuition and your emotions, and become the observer of your energy. Commit to routines of meditation that help you honor and feel your co-creative power. Find the delicate balance between having just enough boundaries to protect your energy but not so many that you keep out the magic and serendipity of the Universe. Be open to this Full Moon helping you expand your consciousness and realize your potential as an energetic being. You are the Universe. Let it move through you and help you manifest everything that is already yours.

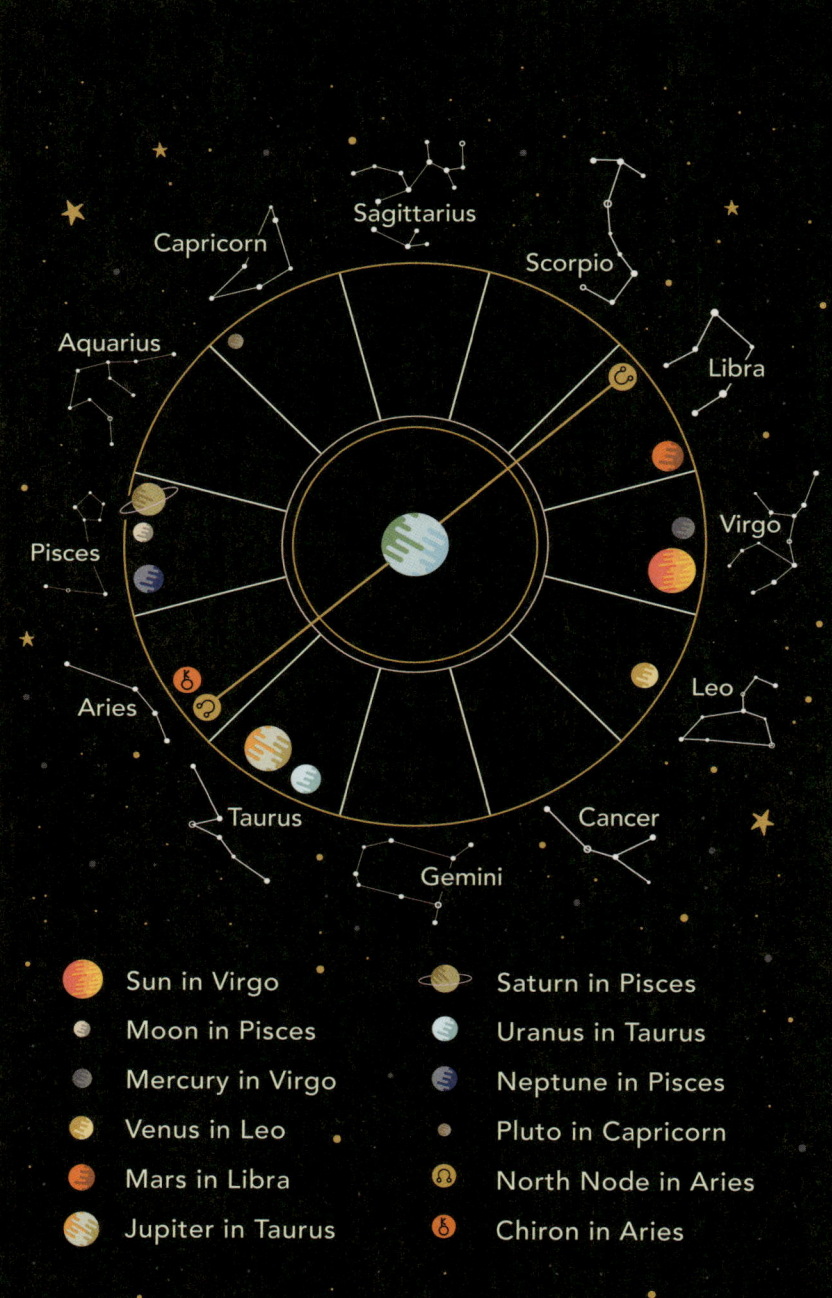

Sun in Virgo

Moon in Pisces

Mercury in Virgo

Venus in Leo

Mars in Libra

Jupiter in Taurus

Saturn in Pisces

Uranus in Taurus

Neptune in Pisces

Pluto in Capricorn

North Node in Aries

Chiron in Aries

ASPECTS

This Pisces Full Moon is aspected with Saturn, which is currently retrograde. The Moon is conjunct, or next to, Saturn in Pisces, while the Sun in Virgo opposes it. Saturn is the planet of commitments. In Pisces, this planet softens a bit but still brings our attention to responsible action. Pisces is the sign of visions and helps us access our dreams. When we align with Pisces, we connect with and download our visionary intuition. We can feel and intuit the life we are meant to live and understand the deeper meaning of it. We also can start to see the bigger picture of our life past the details that tend to absorb our attention.

Saturn in Pisces helps bring form to our dreams and visions. When we align with the higher vibrations of this transit, we can clearly see the steps needed to make our visions tangible. Having dreams is wonderful, but we can easily get stuck in the dream phase of our plans. Saturn helps us understand concrete ways to build our dreams and manifest our visions in reality. With Saturn, though, there are always lessons to be learned. This planet wants to teach us and often takes on a parental role, pointing out where we are not living up to our potential. Saturn in Pisces can feel like pressure on our energy, as it asks us to make choices we may not feel ready to make.

As Saturn impacts this Full Moon, it brings some definition with its energy. It wants you to learn about yourself, your visions, and your plans this Full Moon. It wants you to make commitments that take your dreams out of your head and into the world. This energy may feel overwhelming at times, or it may feel like you cannot fully align with the Pisces energy of this Moon. Pisces tends to make you feel like you are floating away into the ethers. This vibration can be quite lovely, but with Saturn's influence, there is energetic encouragement to remain grounded and connect with your body.

The way to work with Saturn's energy this Full Moon, is to be open to it. If you feel pressure to make a choice or decision, take a deep breath and let yourself relax. Then be open to guidance from Saturn or the place within you that aligns with Saturn's energy. You can even look to the sign of your Saturn placement for some direction. Remember, Saturn wants to teach, so be open to its teaching this Full Moon in often unexpected places.

Saturn's influence this Full Moon also provides a healing element. While Saturn is not known as a healer of the zodiac, Pisces and Virgo are known for their healing abilities. Saturn helps you clearly face where you need healing, forgiveness, and release to bring your visions into form. It also helps you recognize where you may be self-sabotaging out of fear of commitment or an attachment to the past. Again, there are lessons to be learned this Full Moon, and Saturn is your teacher. Become aware of emotions that need to be helped, processed, and shifted for you to move forward. Look at where you are reacting from past experiences to present situations and ask yourself why. Is past pain causing you to react instead of observing the situation? Is past trauma causing you to step out of the present and rely on conditioned patterns?

Allow Saturn to show you where some work may need to be done this Full Moon. Let it illuminate where you are holding yourself back from fully committing to your visions. Align with the Full Moon to release attachments and heal your energy from the past. You may not be able to accomplish this all in one day, but at least make a commitment to yourself on how you will work on healing areas of yourself that keep you in the past or prevent you from taking steps into your future. Keep aligning with Pisces to help you observe yourself and understand the larger vision of your energy. Feel the truth of your vibration this Full Moon, then align with Saturn on how to materialize that truth in physical forms.

HOUSESCOPES

Are you wondering how this Full Moon will affect you directly? While the Full Moon in Pisces will affect us all, we can look more specifically at where we will feel this energy most intensely through understanding our houses. Astrological houses represent areas of our lives. We each have twelve houses shown in our natal charts. One or two astrological signs govern each house. We all have a house, or piece of a house, governed by Pisces. This house tells us which area of our life we will feel the effects of this Full Moon. It also directs our attention to areas where we can shift our energy and look for lower vibrations of Pisces to release. Below is a guide on how to work with this Full Moon depending on which house is ruled by Pisces in your chart. You can look your chart up at astro-charts.com.

FIRST HOUSE PISCES

The First House governs how you project yourself to the world. It directs what you allow others to see and what remains hidden for only you to know. With Pisces here, everyone can see your sensitivity, softness, and psychic gifts. You may even be known as a great healer, with others seeking out your help. You may also find it difficult to draw clear boundaries with others and must work to separate your energy from those around you. On the Full Moon, expect to have your gifts of healing and intuition heightened, but also expect everyone to see them more intensely. Prepare yourself with clear boundaries, and uphold them when needed.

SECOND HOUSE PISCES:

The Second House governs your relationships to resources, including finances and possessions. It also directs your self-worth and ability to create abundance. With Pisces here, you are fluid with your finances, understanding that you create your own abundance. Once you realize your inherent power to attract resources with your energy, you have no trouble calling in everything you need to feel secure. You don't need much to feel supported, though, or to feel worthy. On the Full Moon, let go of anything that feels constrictive around resources or abundance. Encourage yourself to feel like you already have everything you need and trust in your ability to attract it.

THIRD HOUSE PISCES:

The Third House governs your communication and how you exchange information. It directs how you receive energy and give it back to the world. With Pisces here, your creativity takes over when expressing yourself to the world. Your imagination is great, and you use it to craft poetry, music, stories, and other works of art. You are highly observant and infuse your understanding of what you see into your work. On the Full Moon, release anything that holds you back from freely creating. Let go of impulses to hide your talents and allow them to shine through any doubt.

FOURTH HOUSE PISCES:

The Fourth House governs your home, family, and subjective world. It directs your attention to your physical home and the internal home of your energy. With Pisces here, you understand that the Universe is your home. You feel at ease almost anywhere and view your friends as your family. You may spend hours within your own inner landscape, daydreaming, and creating within your mind. Feel how time alone with your dreams nourishes you and restores your energy when the world feels like too much. On the Full Moon, practice forgiveness of yourself and others around you. Release any regret and open the path to connecting more deeply with your heart.

HOUSESCOPES

FIFTH HOUSE PISCES:

The Fifth House governs your creative expression, your inner child, and your ability to have fun. It directs you in enjoying life and your relationship with play. With Pisces here, you have a vast imagination and find it easy to enjoy yourself. You must be careful not to use recreational activities to escape from your reality instead of enhancing it. You need to have hobbies and activities outside of your work that reconnect you with the wonder you felt as a child. On the Full Moon, reveal ways you practice escapism and ask yourself what you are trying to avoid. Feel your power to heal, and know that in accessing your inner child, you often find wounds that need love and care.

SIXTH HOUSE PISCES:

The Sixth House governs your service to the world. It directs how you give your talents to others and what makes you feel fulfilled. With Pisces here, you feel your mission is to help others on their spiritual journey. This path requires you first to walk your own spiritual path. You may go through significant transformations at a young age and be exposed to different philosophies to help you understand your journey. You then apply your knowledge to help others evolve through spiritual growth. On the Full Moon, release any feelings that you are not good enough. You can work on yourself while helping others with their path.

SEVENTH HOUSE PISCES:

The Seventh House governs your relationships and partnerships. It directs how you interact with intimate partners and find harmony in union. With Pisces here, you tend to merge with another. You must be careful to choose partners who share your imagination and creativity, or you may end up feeling lost in their energy. You also need to be aware of codependent relationships where you lose your sense of self and allow another's energy to take over yours. When in healthy relationship, though, you thrive. Knowing that another supports you helps you trust yourself and fearlessly step into your highest visions. On the Full Moon, bring balance to any relationship that does not feel supportive. This may mean letting go of someone or redefining the partnership.

EIGHTH HOUSE PISCES:

The Eighth House governs your personal growth and transformation. It directs the lessons you learn throughout your life and how you apply them. With Pisces here, you are brought many opportunities for spiritual growth and evolution. You welcome any chance to transform your energy and easily shift into a new vibration. You understand the natural cycles and order of the Universe, not getting attached to them. On the Full Moon, release anything that distracts you from your growth. Practice detaching yourself from the mundane attributes of life, and instead step into magic.

NINTH HOUSE PISCES:

The Ninth House governs how you integrate new knowledge and perceptions. It directs your travel and what you seek to broaden your horizons. With Pisces here, you crave expansion. You know there is no limit to how far you would travel to understand the energy of the Universe. You also know that you are already connected to everything and only need to travel as far as yourself. Still, you crave new lands and new energies. On the Full Moon, release any regrets for things you could have done. Know there is always time to experience the world the way you want over many lifetimes. If you can, spend time by the ocean and allow your mind to drift into new territories.

HOUSESCOPES

TENTH HOUSE PISCES:

The Tenth House governs your career and reputation. It directs what part of yourself you show to the world. It also directs your commitments and responsibilities. With Pisces here, you may have trouble committing to one course of action. You like options and possibilities. You may even rebel if you feel constricted by your work or responsibilities. It's best to find a career that gives you the freedom to express your imagination and creativity. You also do well when working for yourself unencumbered by corporate life and traditional work hours. On the Full Moon, release any pressure you may have put on yourself to conform to a traditional career. Instead, allow your intuition to lead you to your true purpose.

ELEVENTH HOUSE PISCES:

The Eleventh House rules our relationship with humanity. It directs how we interact with others, including our community and less intimate friends. The Eleventh House is our outer circle of friends, where the Seventh and Fourth Houses are our inner circle. With Pisces here, you belong to spiritual communities, intent on uplifting the world through higher consciousness. You may understand philosophies that many aren't familiar with yet, but you also know it's your work to teach them. On the Full Moon, release anything that holds you back from sharing your spiritual understanding with others. Instead, embrace your knowledge and trust that others in your community will too.

TWELFTH HOUSE PISCES:

Pisces traditionally governs the Twelfth House. It shares many attributes with the sign. It directs our spiritual path and growth. With Pisces here, you are spiritually wise beyond your years. You may even take your knowledge for granted, assuming everyone understands the world as you do. Your wisdom can also make you feel isolated, as you see the world differently than others. Be gentle with yourself and allow yourself to unfold. On the Full Moon, release any pressure you put on yourself to have it all figured out. Instead, embrace your path and have compassion for yourself.

PISCES LUNAR FLOW

Pisces rules the feet and our connection with walking the Earth. Traditionally thought of as the fish, this aspect of Pisces reminds us of the primordial sea we came from and the process of evolution, which allowed us to walk on land. Pisces energy in its purest form returns us to the sea and invokes all the properties of water. Since most of us can't float away into space, we need to reaffirm our connection with the Earth through our feet in order to stay present in our lives., This connection will keep us anchored in reality and deepen our connection with the dreamlike state of this Pisces Full Moon.

During any Full Moon, it's good to move your body. You want your yoga practice to be fluid, uplifting, and capable of moving any stagnant energy so that you are free to shift your energy. The following sequence will move your energy while keeping you grounded in your feet.

SEATED SEQUENCE

Come up to a cross-legged position. With your spine upright, make circles in your hips, rolling your torso around. Continue this for about 30 seconds, then switch directions. Feel the fluid movement of your body.

Come back to center and interlace your hands behind your head. On inhale, twist to the right. On exhale, twist to the left. Do this for 1 minute, then release.

Still seated, place your hands on your knees, then arch and round your back. Feel the full undulation of your spine as it waves back and forth. Feel even your neck and throat open as you arch your spine. Continue for a minute, then return to stillness.

CAT/COW TO DOWNWARD-FACING DOG

Come onto your hands and knees, then arch your back on inhale; round it on exhale. Again, feel the wave of your spine and the fluidity of your movement. Continue for a minute. Come back to center and roll through your rib cage, making large circles with your torso. Continue for 30 seconds before switching sides. There is no right or wrong way to do these, just move organically and in tune with your body. Come back to center and exhale into Downward Dog.

SUN SALUTATION A - 5 ROUNDS

Stand at the top of your mat. Inhale, stretch your arms overhead > Exhale, fold forward > Inhale, lengthen out your back > Exhale, step back to Plank Pose and lower > Inhale, reach your chest up for Cobra Pose, legs on the ground > Exhale, Downward Dog Pose. Stay here for 5 breaths and feel your entire body expand. On exhale, step to the top of the mat > Inhale, lengthen through your spine > Exhale, fold forward > Inhale, come up to standing, reaching arms overhead > Exhale, hands to your heart. Pause for a moment and feel yourself centered throughout your body. *On your fifth round, remain in Downward Dog and breathe for 5 breaths.

LUNGE > WARRIOR 2 > GODDESS POSE

From Downward Dog, step your left foot forward into a Lunge Pose. Your back heel will lift from the ground and your leg will stay straight. Bend deeply into your front knee as you tilt your tailbone toward the ground. Reach your arms to the sky and send your breath into your

PISCES LUNAR FLOW

hips. After 5 breaths, open up into Warrior 2. Spin your back foot flat on the ground in a 45-degree angle inward and rotate your torso to the right side of the mat, reaching your arms to either side. Bend in your front knee, pressing it out to the left. Take 5 breaths here, opening up your pelvis and grounding down through your legs. Inhale, straighten your leg, and bring your feet to parallel in a wide-legged stance. Turn your toes out to a 45-degree angle and bend in your knees for Goddess Pose. Bend your arms by your sides with your palms facing the sky. Breathe here for 5 breaths as you feel your feet root into the ground. Once complete, straighten your legs, rotate your right foot out, repeat Warrior 2 and Lunge on this side. From Warrior 2, release your hands to the ground and step back through a vinyasa or straight to Downward Dog.

WARRIOR 2 > REVERSE WARRIOR > EXTEND WARRIOR FLOW

From Downward Dog, step your left foot forward into Warrior 2, then rotate your left palm to the sky and arch back for Reverse Warrior. Reach your left arm in line with your ear and stretch open the left side of your body. Feel the play of opening as you bend deeper into the front knee and reach with your arm. Spend 5 breaths here, then bring your torso upright and place your left elbow on your front knee for Extended Warrior. Reach your right arm overhead in line with your ear and take 5 breaths here. On inhale, lift your torso upright and reach back into Reverse Warrior, then exhale and come back into Extended Warrior. Flow like this for 5 breaths, inhaling into Reverse Warrior, exhaling in Extended Warrior. Feel the energy moving with each inhale and exhale. After 5 rounds, switch sides with your right foot forward (you'll also return to facing the front of the mat). After this side, return to Downward Dog either through a vinyasa or by stepping back.

MALASANA (SQUAT POSE)

Hop your feet forward to the outside of your hands with your feet hips' width apart or wider, with your toes slightly turned out. Drop your hips down for a Squat Pose. Press firmly through the outer edges of your feet and feel your heels energetically draw together. If your heels lift from the ground, place a blanket beneath them or sit on a block until your hips begin to release. Take 5 deep breaths here, allowing your hips to open as your feet root into the Earth. Release into a forward bend, hanging over your legs as your spine releases.

BADDHA KONASANA

Come to a seated position and take the soles of your feet together, knees out to either side. Grab hold of your feet, slightly pressing on the inside arches. Inhale as you lengthen through your spine. Exhale, fold over your legs, and breathe here for 5 to 10 breaths. Feel each inhale extend down into your hips, opening them, and your exhales relax your entire nervous system.

SAVASANA

Stretch both your legs out long on the mat and place your palms facing upward in a receptive motion. Feel your entire body supported by the ground beneath you. Let your breath become natural and feel the energy circulating through you from your practice.

Visit spiritdaughter.com/collections/zodiac-yoga to flow with our Pisces Zodiac Yoga video.

PISCES MEDITATION

Pisces is the most spiritual sign of the zodiac, and her energy reminds us that we are spiritual beings in a human form. This Full Moon is a time to practice our most observant self and, instead of reacting to sensations that arise within, watch them and let them pass. This observation is the heart of mindfulness meditation, which starts by observing the feelings that exist in each area of the body. Through placing our awareness methodically on each part of our bodies, we are holding space for sensations and emotions to be felt, seen, and released. The purpose of this meditation is to train the conscious and subconscious mind to merely observe events internally or externally, not react to them. True observation is an art form— one that needs time, commitment, and understanding. The following meditation will provide a foundation for this type of awareness. Practice it on the day of the Full Moon, but also try to incorporate it into a daily practice to help build your powers of observation and non-reactivity.

BODY SCAN - 15 MINUTES

Throughout this practice, place your attention on one area of your body. Become completely immersed in the sensations that arise in this area. When focused on an area, pay no attention to the rest of your body. Let all other sensations, including your thoughts, fade into the background. As you focus on different places, feel all the sensations of that area. These sensations can be tingling, heat, coolness, pain, or even emotions. If you feel nothing at all, this is ok too. Just keep your awareness on the area. If thoughts or feelings arise, let them pass like the rest of the sensations. Give them no attention, not even to block them. Just let them go.

Lie in a comfortable position, relaxing your entire body. Feel the ground beneath you, supporting you. Release any tension from your neck, shoulders, and face. Take three deep breaths, exhaling from your mouth. With each exhale, relax even more. Allow your breathing to return to normal. Begin the body scans with the crown of your head. Spend a few breaths here, observing what arises in this area. Be genuinely curious about what may be residing at the crown of your head. Watch the sensations as if you are watching a movie. If it helps to keep your concentration, you can try labeling the sensations as if you are filing them away. Resist the natural tendency to judge or evaluate these sensations. There are no good or bad feelings here—only what is happening in the present moment.

Continue moving through your body, placing your attention in different areas. Move from your head to your face, neck, shoulders, arms, hands, torso, pelvis, legs, and feet. Cover your entire body with your attention piece by piece. Spend only a few breaths on each area, not dwelling on the sensations. As you give your body and energy attention, it will be able to release. Letting go is first a process of awareness. We need to become aware of what we are releasing before we can truly let it go from our energy. This meditation will help sharpen your attention while limiting your reactivity. If you react to sensations, they are more likely to stay. It is through conscious acknowledgment without reaction that the sensations pass.

As we train our minds with the Body Scan, we also teach ourselves how to not react to situations outside the body. We extend the practice and become observers of our emotions rather than letting our emotions control us. We begin to encompass the true energy of Pisces, who allows all things to pass through her energy to be either released or transmuted. We eventually learn not to hold onto any energy and understand everything is temporary.

FULL MOON RITUALS

The following are rituals you can practice this Full Moon, along with the practices in the workbook. You can do any or all of them. It's best to practice within 48 hours of the Full Moon exact to receive the complete magic of this lunar cycle phase.

HOLD A FULL MOON CIRCLE

You can set up a Full Moon circle for yourself or for a group. This circle can be inside or outside. It can contain as many or as few objects as you like. Use your intuition when setting up a circle. Below are suggestions on how to set up and hold a Full Moon circle.

+ Begin by opening yourself to guidance from yourself and the Universe by saying "I am open to guidance."

+ Set the perimeter of your circle with crystals and candles. Use crystals for Pisces and Virgo. These include Amethyst, Aquamarine, Apatite, Labradorite for Pisces, and Smokey Quartz, Azurite, Jade, Unakite, and Pink Calcite for Virgo.

AMETHYST   AQUAMARINE   APATITE   LABRADORITE

SMOKEY QUARTZ   AZURITE   UNAKITE   PINK CALCITE

+ Set the center of the circle with a large crystal, crystal grid, or candle. If using a crystal grid, create it in a circular or spiral shape with a sphere in the center to represent the Water element.

+ Once the perimeter is set, visualize a white light encasing the circle, providing both protection and purification.

+ Cleanse the circle with a dried herb bundle. Lavender is an excellent herb for Pisces. You can use it as a bundle or loose in a bowl. Fan the smoke from the herb around the circle, starting in the most easterly point and moving clockwise.

+ Before you our your guests sit in the circle, cleanse them and yourself from head to toe. Once you have all entered the circle, pause for a moment to let the energy settle before you begin.

+ Begin with each member introducing themself. Talk about the astrological energy of the day and how it is affecting each one of you. Share and learn from each other about your unique experiences with this Full Moon.

+ Practice the yoga and meditation in this book.

+ Complete the practices in this book after discussing the content.

+ Talk more about your experiences with the practices and do the card-reading practice.

+ Close the circle by giving gratitude to everyone who chooses to honor the Full Moon with you. Give thanks both to the elements for supporting you and the energy of the Universe for guiding you along the way.

FULL MOON RITUALS

MOON BATH

You can include a Moon bathing ritual alongside your circle or alone. If you are practicing it within the circle, include it during the meditation practice. You can also include a second session of Moon bathing after you've completed the practices as a way to process the knowledge you learned and integrate it into your energetic field.

Moon bathing is a simple practice. Much like sunbathing, it allows you to absorb the energy and light of the Sun reflected from the Moon. It can create a sense of calm within you and help you feel connected to your intuition as the fluctuations of your mind settle.

+ Find a space outside that allows you to lie directly in the Moon's light.

+ Set out a blanket or lie directly on the Earth.

+ You can practice this with clothes on or off. You can even practice it in a bathing suit.

+ Lie under the Moon with the palms of your hands up in a receptive position.

+ Spend 20 to 60 minutes under the Moon. You can listen to a meditation or meditate on your own.

+ Absorb the light of the Moon and allow it to soothe your soul.

+ Bonus practice: Place four pieces of Quartz around you to amplify the energy of the Moon: one above your head, one below your feet, and one to each side.

+ Bonus practice: Place a piece of Quartz in a jar of water and place it beside you to create Moon water. You can use this water in your next bath to continue absorbing the Moon's energy.

+ Complete your Moon bath by thanking the Moon for her light.

PISCES CARD READING

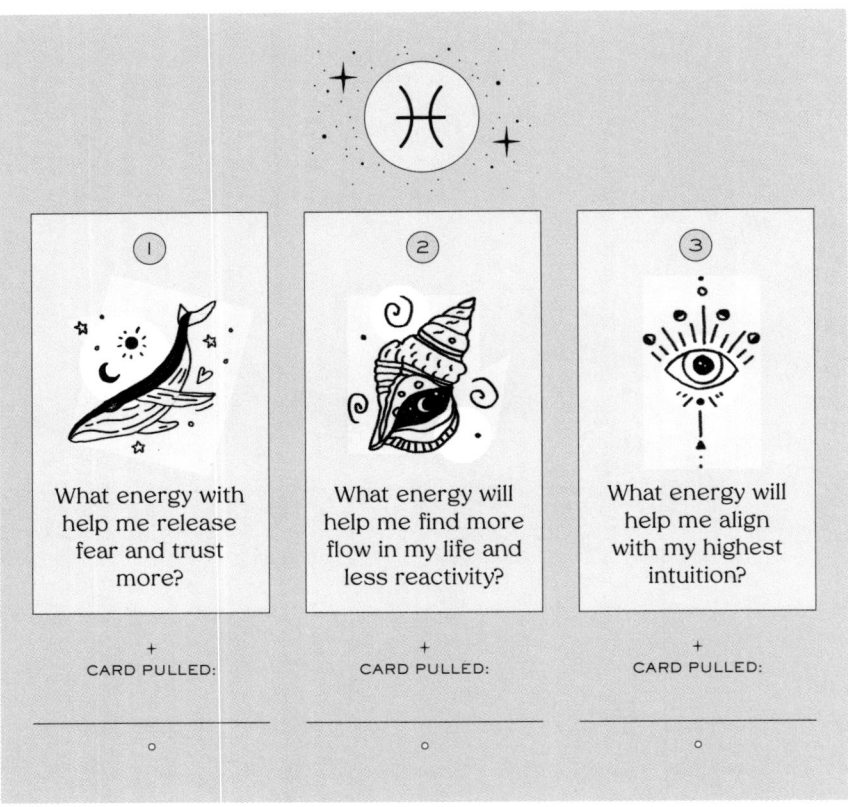

1

What energy with help me release fear and trust more?

CARD PULLED:

_____

2

What energy will help me find more flow in my life and less reactivity?

CARD PULLED:

_____

3

What energy will help me align with my highest intuition?

CARD PULLED:

_____

Reading Cards is a beautiful way to access your intuition and tap into your, and the Universe's, higher wisdom. Anyone can pull cards, as long as you are willing to receive the information they provide. You need no prior experience, or training, just an open and clear mind.

You may use any cards you like for this practice, including but not limited to: Tarot Cards, Animal Medicine Cards, Oracle Cards or any Affirmation Cards. You also can pull cards from a few decks to gain different perspectives. If you are new to card pulling, try to ask only one deck the same question, as asking different decks the same question can become quite confusing. Below are some general guidelines on how to pull cards. Please improvise as needed and above anything else, listen to your intuition.

CLEAR YOUR MIND
A settled, grounded mind is essential for pulling cards. The last thing you want is random thoughts running around when you are trying to receive clear answers from yourself. Practice the breath work and meditation in this workbook to prepare and settle your mind. You may also clear your mind using sound frequencies through singing bowls. These can either be crystal or metal bowls. Play the bowl, or bowls, for about 3-5 minutes to help rid your mind of external noise as you focus on the harmony of the sound.

PISCES CARD READING

PICK YOUR DECK
There are many different decks out there. You can choose as many as you like. Know, though, that they each provide you a different energy or medicine. Tarot Cards are the most popular and should be used carefully. Although very useful, Tarot cards can give the wrong impression if you interpret them harshly. Animal Medicine cards offer different types of messages from the animal realm which can help align with the spirit of nature. These cards give you the medicine you need to apply to your situation or question. Affirmation cards provide you with guidance in the form of words or phrases. When reading these cards, it is best to meditate on what the affirmation means for you. It is also helpful to repeat the affirmation a few times and see how it makes you feel. There are many other cards you can experiment with, like Goddess Cards, Angel Cards, and so on. The important thing to remember with any card is that they each have different angles and sides. There are often a few interpretations of the same card.

SHUFFLE
Shuffle the cards the easiest way for you. Some cards are smaller and can be shuffled like a regular deck of playing cards, while others with take some effort. If all else fails, spread them out on the floor in front of you then regather them. Keep a clear mind while shuffling. You can also repeat " I am open to receiving guidance and intuition." Refrain from asking your questions until the next step.

PISCES CARD QUESTIONS
You are free to ask the deck any questions you need answers to on this Blue Moon. The following questions are meant to help you harness the energy of Pisces through the cards to clarify some of these energies in your mind. This is a three-part card reading, where you'll ask the deck three questions. Before beginning, spread your freshly shuffled cards in a wide arc in front of you. Use your left middle finger to choose the card, first waving your hand slowly over the cards. You'll feel a magnetic pull, or slight tingle, in your fingertip when you hover over the right card. Chose one card at a time, taking a moment to breathe in between questions. Keep the cards flipped over until you pull all three.

What energy with help me release fear and trust more?

What energy will help me find more flow in my life and less reactivity?

What energy will help me align with my highest intuition?

TAKE THEM IN
Once you have your cards, flip them over. Before looking up their meaning, sit with them for a moment and allow them to speak to you. Intuit your own meaning and interpretation of the card. What is the card trying to tell you? What are you trying to tell yourself? After a few moments with the cards, look up their meaning. Sit with that information, merging it with your intuitive meaning of the cards.

As with everything, enjoy this process. Do not worry if you are doing it right or wrong. Just follow your intuition, and trust the journey. Accept the cards you are dealt and use their energy wisely to help guide you when you need it the most.

PISCES PRACTICES

Notes on healing:

one step backward can
create two steps forward

healing happens in moments

give yourself time

give the time some time

- spirit daughter

The journey of this Pisces Full Moon is one of trust—trust in yourself, your intuition, and the overall flow of your life. Once you reach this state of trust and surrender, your consciousness can expand free from the limitation of doubt. You realize your infinite connections to everything in the Universe. You also learn to trust your life's journey, no matter how many twists and turns it brings you. You understand the deeper meaning of everything, even the events that cause you pain and heartbreak. Everything becomes part of the story your energy is here to live.

When we realize our potential as energetic beings, our life shifts to include more magic and mystical encounters. We step in our rhythm, and it seems the Universe is orchestrating our life for us. Pisces reminds us that we are the Universe, and the Universe is us. When we have an intuitive breakthrough, or we see an apparent sign, it's our higher Self giving us the information. When we say the Universe is supporting us, we are supporting ourselves. Pisces teaches us that everything is made of the same energy. Our energy is contained within our individual field, but it is still connected to all energy. This connection is where consciousness lies, and when we become aware of it, it brings us infinite knowledge.

PISCES PRACTICES

When we tap into the universal knowledge held within each of us, our life's direction becomes clear. The answers appear in front of us, and we realize that everything we desire is already ours. When we trust our intuitive knowledge, we do not need proof or evidence. We confidently hear it and follow it, knowing that it will guide us to what our energy needs for its soul journey. This doesn't mean our intuition keeps everything easy for us or pain-free. It can sometimes lead us to the most trying circumstances to help us grow. Remember, our energy is here in this manifestation to evolve. This evolution is not always comfortable, and it's not always what our conscious mind wants. This process is where trust comes in. Pisces teaches us to trust our journey, even when it doesn't make sense. Trust that you are experiencing what you need to evolve, and trust that it will all make sense one day or one lifetime.

In working with our intuition, we need to recognize that we do not live in a world that supports it. Most people want logical reasoning, explainable analysis, and evidence that our intuition is correct. Intuitive knowledge, though, does not work this way. Often, we must follow it before having any proof that it is accurate. This trust is the makings of leaps of faith, where we don't know where the road will lead or if it even exists. Living by your intuition asks you to get comfortable saying, "I don't have any evidence this is true, but I trust it's correct," or "I don't know why I know this. I just do." The world is not set up for these statements, but the more you take a chance to live by your intuition, you will help shift the systems we have in place that make decisions. Practice relying on your intuition more and more each day. Know that it comes from your higher consciousness, which is connected to the past, present, and future.

Reaching the state of consciousness, which this Pisces Full Moon opens for us, can take years to master. Much like a Buddhist monk on a quest to find enlightenment, the process of connecting to your intuitive knowledge is not something that happens overnight. It begins with small, daily incremental steps that accumulate over time to create significant change in your mind, body, and spirit. It takes dedication to shift consciousness, something the energy of Virgo can help us accomplish. This Full Moon combines the powers of Pisces to inspire us to view the Universe as a vast energetic system and Virgo to help us maintain a daily practice that grounds our energy so we feel safe to explore alternative realities.

Virgo is the container for the exploration encouraged by Pisces. This container is flexible, though, and can change with time. A manifestation of this container may be a daily meditation practice to help you connect with your intuition. One week, this practice may occur at 7 a.m. every day, while another week, it may happen at 8 p.m. The point is, some organization of time can help us create space to connect with our energy. Most of us do not have all day to sit with the Universe, unobstructed by mundane tasks. We are householders who have responsibilities and need organized space for our mystical side to wander. If we do, though, provide ourselves with space to expand our consciousness, our everyday tasks become less daunting. We find our flow and drop into the rhythm of the Universe, the rhythm of us.

The following practices are designed to help you merge the energies of Pisces and Virgo. They help you step away from their lower frequencies and integrate their higher ones. Take your time with these questions, allowing the answers to appear. Receive the answers from your higher consciousness instead of creating them with your lower mind. Trust that they are coming from your intuition, which is connected to the knowledge of the Universe.

PISCES PRACTICES

1. How can you carve out time in your life to explore your energetic field?

_____

_____

_____

_____

_____

_____

_____

_____

_____

_____

_____

_____

_____

2. What grounds your energy and relieves anxious thoughts, freeing you to explore your consciousness?

_____

_____

_____

_____

_____

_____

_____

_____

_____

_____

_____

_____

PISCES PRACTICES

3. Are there parts of yourself that need healing? How can you energetically heal? Meaning, How can you energetically detach yourself from your past?

_____

_____

_____

_____

_____

_____

_____

_____

_____

_____

_____

_____

_____

4. Are you familiar with energy medicine, such as acupuncture, Reiki, and cranio-sacral therapy, among others. Do any of these speak to you for healing? How can you create a schedule of healing that makes it a priority in your life?

_____

_____

_____

_____

_____

_____

PISCES PRACTICES

5. What allows you to hear your intuition?

_____

_____

_____

_____

_____

_____

_____

_____

_____

_____

_____

_____

_____

_____

_____

6. When you do hear your intuition, do you follow it? Or do doubts come up? What prevents you from listening to it?

_____

_____

_____

_____

_____

_____

_____

_____

_____

_____

PISCES PRACTICES

7. Do you overly rely on analysis and logical reasoning, which dampen your intuition? Do you rely on these things out of mistrust of yourself or the need to have the perfect answer?

8. What are some situations when your intuition was correct, even if you didn't follow it? Begin to build evidence for yourself that you can trust your intuition.

_____

_____

_____

_____

_____

_____

_____

_____

_____

_____

_____

9. Begin to become more aware of the infinite energetic connections around you. What signs have you experienced? What coincidences have occurred, linking two separate events together? What serendipity have you experienced?

_____

_____

_____

_____

_____

_____

_____

_____

PISCES PRACTICES

10. Begin to see yourself as an energetic being. What weighs your energy down? What drains it? What makes you feel lighter? What gives you energy?

LAST QUARTER: IN GEMINI

The Last Quarter Moon occurs when the Moon makes it to the last quarter of the lunar cycle, completing her journey around the Earth back to the Sun. On the Last Quarter Moon, we see a Half Moon in our sky, signifying a 90-degree separation, or square aspect, between the Sun and the Moon. Squares bring up friction and often crises in the energetic body. They feel tense to us, and we can choose to either resist them or work with the energy presented. If we do choose to lean into the energy and opportunity of the Last Quarter, we tap into a powerful force of release. The Last Quarter Moon's energy encourages us to surrender to what we cannot control and let go as we make space for new energy. There is often an epiphany at this stage of the lunar cycle, when we realize the person we can become if we can finally release an old pattern, emotion, or attachment.

The journey of the Last Quarter is not always an easy one; we must be willing to confront places of resistance within ourselves. These are the areas that hold on to energies that are no longer serving our highest visions. We may feel a loss during this time, or even some grief for the things we are releasing. Embrace these feelings, knowing they are part of the process of transformation. Also know that in order to call in new energies, you must let go of the things that block you or lower your frequency, even if they feel comfortable. Trust the process of your release and embrace the witness consciousness to help you through this time.

Gemini flavors this Last Quarter with the Moon being positioned in her stars and the Sun still in Virgo. Gemini and Virgo are both ruled by the planet Mercury, who tends to quicken our minds and our energy. Take time to feel grounded this day as your mind races or if anxious energy tries to take over. Utilize breathing techniques to center yourself and steady your vibration as we move through this Moon.

Gemini gives us the gift of survey. Her energy compels us to look at every aspect of our lives and take stock. Gemini is an Air energy and allows us to see the different pieces of our lives along with the bigger picture. She fuels our curiosity and helps open our minds to new possibilities and perspectives. Align with Gemini this Last Quarter to question how different energies, situations, people, and projects are fitting together in the intricate web that is you. For the pieces that don't seem to be aligning, decide to either adjust them or release them with ease. Feel into your intuition this Last Quarter with the help of the Sun still in Virgo to decide where to continue to work and where to create space for new energies to enter. Try not to overthink this process. Feel the element of Air helping you flow freely through the pieces of your life while being open to what new adventures may be around the corner.

> What are you willing to let go this
> Last Quarter Moon to allow yourself to
> receive new energy?

_____

_____

_____

AFFIRMATIONS

When you think of yourself as an energetic being that is part of the infinite Universe, what words come up to describe yourself? What helps you define a higher state of consciousness?

_____

_____

_____

_____

_____

_____

_____

_____

_____

_____

Take the words from above and create powerful "I am" statements to help you shift your vibration over time. You can create these affirmations from one of the words or two. Repeat them each day, knowing the repetition changes your frequency over time.

_____

_____

_____

_____

_____

_____

_____

HAPPY
FULL MOON!

Thank you to everyone who supported and purchased this workbook.

Special Thanks to Rebecca Reitz (rebeccareitz.com, @becca_reitz) for her beautiful artwork on the cover & pages 2, 4, 10, 13, 16, 30.

For a monthly subscription contact hello@spiritdaughter.com or visit www.spiritdaughter.com.

Disclaimer: The exercises and yoga sequences in this book are physical activities that should be performed carefully to avoid injury. You agree to accept all risks and release Spirit Daughter and any guest instructors from any and all liabilities. Please take care and enjoy.

Follow along our journey on IG:
@spiritdaughter

We always love seeing your photos & hearing about your experiences with the workbooks! Tag us to be featured on our community page:
@spiritdaughtercollective

For more information contact:
hello@spiritdaughter.com.

First paperback edition July 2023

Book design by Rebecca Reitz
Cover design by Rebecca Reitz

ISBN 978-1-960013-28-6 (paperback)

www.spiritdaughter.com